COMMUNICATING IN WRITING AND THROUGH PRESENTATIONS

Self-coaching questions, inspiration, tips, and practical exercises for becoming an awesome manager

⌘

Managerial Competencies Series
Playbook No. 5

CÉLESTE GRIMARD

Copyright © 2018 Céleste Grimard, Canada

All rights reserved. All materials on these pages are copyrighted by Céleste Grimard. Reproduction, modification, storage of all or part of this book in a retrieval system or retransmission, in any form or by any means, electronic, mechanical, or otherwise is strictly prohibited without prior written permission from the author. Although every effort has been made to indicate the sources of text and ideas, it's possible that we missed some! If you're aware of references or citations that haven't been provided, please contact the author. This book doesn't constitute legal advice and isn't a substitute for independent professional advice.

ISBN-13: 978-1979023412

CreateSpace, Charleston, SC USA

⌘
ACKNOWLEDGMENTS

I originally developed this series as a self-study, self-paced program for hundreds of managers working in a geographically dispersed area. Over the span of many years, these awesome managers offered me feedback, inspiration, and encouragement to transform this program into a series of practical, easy to read books accessible to all managers. Thank you! I also sincerely thank Rhiannon Ward for her assistance in editing and proofreading the books in this series.

CONTENTS

Series Introduction   1

Introduction   3

1. Reality Check: Self-Coaching Questions   7

2. Inspiring Your Journey   13

3. Tips for Awesome Managers   18

4. Dilemmas: What Would You Do?   55

5. Planning For Action   65

About the Managerial Competencies Series   67

References   92

COMMUNICATING IN WRITING AND THROUGH PRESENTATIONS

Welcome to the Managerial Competencies Series!

The aim of this series is to help you understand and build the core competencies you need to become an awesome manager.

There's no getting around it. There are tons of journals, books, blogs, videos – you name it – on the topic of management. Yes, a lot has been written and said about how to be an effective manager. Everyone has their own spin to put on this topic, and research studies on this topic are practically endless. How does

COMMUNICATING IN WRITING AND THROUGH PRESENTATIONS

a busy manager sort through all the fads and fashions to find the nuggets of wisdom?

In designing this series, I pored over loads of resources and talked with hundreds of managers. I set aside all the fashions, fads, and fantasies, and I extracted only what is likely to be of enduring value to you. Although this series is geared towards practical, immediate use, I hope that it will provoke you to think deeply about managing and your role as a manager, and that it will make a difference for you so you can make a difference for others.

This module – Communicating in Writing and Through Presentations – is fifth of 15 books, each covering a key competency of awesome managers. **Turn to page 55 to learn more about this series**, including the full slate of books, how each book is structured, and tips on how to get the most out of them.

Throughout the book, I will refer to your **learning journal** and your **feedback team**. **These helpful tools are explained on page 82.**

Communicating in Writing and Through Presentations: INTRODUCTION

Awesome managers communicate their ideas effectively, whether orally or in writing.

COMMUNICATING IN WRITING AND THROUGH PRESENTATIONS

Oral and written communications are central to managerial work. Your competencies in both areas determine how well you're able to influence the decision-making process and motivate and direct the work of others. Managers must be able to communicate their ideas, proposals, decisions, and findings in a capable manner. Thus, rather than being "frills," effective writing and making presentations are at the core of managerial work.

Although most people would agree that the ability to make effective presentations is important, the same can't be said about effective writing. Sometimes, people argue that effective writing is such a basic skill that it belongs in high school or in an English 100 class. Unfortunately, these are often the same people who: (a) have difficulty expressing their ideas in a coherent fashion but don't know it; and (b) don't realize how important this competency is for success in the workplace. It may be that they haven't received adequate

COMMUNICATING IN WRITING AND THROUGH PRESENTATIONS

feedback on their competencies in this area (due to large class sizes, etc.) and, as a result, lack the sense of "conscious incompetence" that is needed to motivate them to pay attention to their writing. Without this awareness and motivation, it's hard for such individuals to appreciate the need for improvement regardless of the feedback that they may receive from "helpful critics." This problem will only create bigger problems for them.

Business writers Phil Hunsaker and Tony Alessandra argue: "You may be bright, ambitious, and hardworking and yet have a handicap that will stall your career climb on the lower rungs of the management ladder: poor writing skills. Writing abilities are as visible as a person's wardrobe, but the impressions you leave through your written work last even longer." If your writing and presentations come across as professional, then you're more likely to be viewed as a professional. If, on the other

COMMUNICATING IN WRITING AND THROUGH PRESENTATIONS

hand, they are sloppy and awkward, they will reflect badly on you.

Much has been written on both topics. Below is just a small sampling of the abundant resources available online.

Writing Resources:
- grammarly.com/blog/how-to-improve-writing-skills
- grammarbook.com
- cws.illinois.edu/workshop/writers
- owl.english.purdue.edu

Presenting Resources:
- skillsyouneed.com/presentation-skills.html
- ljlseminars.com/monthtip.htm
- students.ubc.ca/career/career-resources/presentation-skills
- forbes.com/sites/forbescoachescouncil/2016/06/13/10-ways-to-improve-your-presentation-skills

COMMUNICATING IN WRITING AND THROUGH PRESENTATIONS

1

REALITY CHECK: SELF COACHING QUESTIONS

To help you examine your communication skills and challenges, we invite you to ask yourself a series of self-coaching questions. While thinking about your behavior in the past six months, find specific examples that support your answers. Consider whether or not

COMMUNICATING IN WRITING AND THROUGH PRESENTATIONS

"counter examples" exist; in other words, times when you may not have behaved in a manner that is consistent with your answer. In answering these questions, think about how you generally are rather than temporary aberrations due to stress or other factors.

Your answers to these self-coaching questions will shine a light on how you see yourself. If you know yourself well, your answers will be right on the mark. However, many people don't have accurate self-perceptions because they're not used to assessing themselves, they feel uncomfortable with the idea of reflecting on their own behaviors, or they truly don't know themselves well. As a result, their answers may be *extremely* inflated or low.

In all cases, but especially when answers are extreme (in any direction), seeking candid and honest feedback from others can be a valuable way of shedding light on your actual competency levels. You can learn a lot more

COMMUNICATING IN WRITING AND THROUGH PRESENTATIONS

about yourself if you get feedback from others.

You can ask people to answer some of the self-coaching questions for you and provide examples or anecdotes of situations that illustrate their answers. They may not tell you what you want to hear, but it may be exactly what you need to help you make progress on your journey toward becoming an awesome manager. As American writer Herbert Sebastian Aga said in his book *A Time for Greatness*, "The truth that makes men free is, for the most part, the truth which men prefer not to hear."

Asking others for feedback takes courage on everyone's part. Others don't necessarily have the same picture of you as you have of yourself, and people are sometimes reluctant to "tell it like it is." However, "feedback-lite" that is polite and tells you what you hope to hear won't help you grow as a person. Tell people that you need the straight goods (politely though!).

COMMUNICATING IN WRITING AND THROUGH PRESENTATIONS

→ Do I consider grammar and spelling when composing emails, memos, and letters?
→ Have I received any feedback about my writing skills? Was it positive or negative?
→ Do I feel confident about my writing abilities?
→ Have I received any feedback about the length of my memos, letters, and/or reports?
→ Do I prefer to deal with all issues in writing?
→ Do I avoid using words and phrases such as: *in terms of, utilize, commensurate with, at your earliest convenience, I am in receipt of, with reference to, until such time as,* or *will you be kind enough*?
→ Do I avoid "double negatives" and other thorny problems? (If you don't know what this is, then the answer may be "No.")
→ Which is more important: the ideas expressed or how they're expressed?
→ Do I feel comfortable preparing and making presentations?

COMMUNICATING IN WRITING AND THROUGH PRESENTATIONS

→ Do I like to "wow" people with a fancy PowerPoint presentation?

→ Do I prepare thoroughly for presentations? Or do I tend to give off-the-cuff speeches so that they come across as being more natural?

→ Do I keep my head up while making presentations? Or, do I tend to read from my notes or the PowerPoint slides?

→ Have people complimented me on my presentation skills?

→ Does my voice have variety and enthusiasm while presenting? Or is it fairly monotone?

→ Do I feel confident when I'm making a presentation? Or am I overcome by nerves?

→ Do I prepare a great deal in advance of giving a presentation?

→ Do I time my presentations well? Or do I often find myself running out of time to cover all my points?

COMMUNICATING IN WRITING AND THROUGH PRESENTATIONS

Reflection

What do your answers say about your perceptions of your communication strengths and opportunities for improvement? Do you feel comfortable communicating? Do you need to pay more attention to preparing, organizing, and delivering presentations? Do you feel confident about your writing skills, or do you need a tune-up? What did your feedback team have to say about your writing and presentation skills?

Whether you think you communicate effectively in any medium or that you have work to do, the important thing is to use this reflection as an opportunity to make improvements ... now!

COMMUNICATING IN WRITING AND THROUGH PRESENTATIONS

2

INSPIRING YOUR JOURNEY

As you read through the following quotations, take note of the ones that speak to you the most. Then consider the message they are conveying to you.

COMMUNICATING IN WRITING AND THROUGH PRESENTATIONS

As soon as you move one step up from the bottom, your effectiveness depends on your ability to reach others through the spoken or written word. - *Peter Drucker*

⌘

You can have brilliant ideas, but if you can't get them across, your ideas won't get you anywhere. - *Lee Iacocca*

⌘

To write simply is as difficult as to be good.
- *W. Somerset Maugham*

⌘

Words are like X-Rays. If you use them properly, they'll go through anything. Read them and you're pierced. - *Aldous Huxley*

⌘

Words are, of course, the most powerful drug used by mankind. - *Rudyard Kipling*

⌘

When talking to the carpenter, use the language of the carpenter. - *Aristotle*

COMMUNICATING IN WRITING AND THROUGH PRESENTATIONS

Tell them what you are going to tell them, tell them, and then tell them what you just told them. - *Unknown, often attributed to Toastmasters*

⌘

The most important thing is to read as much as you can, like I did. It will give you an understanding of what makes good writing and it will enlarge your vocabulary.
- *J. K. Rowling*

⌘

Good writing is like a windowpane.
- *George Orwell*

⌘

The thing about good writing is that it has a music to it. - *Lauren Graham*

⌘

Through an arbitrary problem, I have arrived at a tenet of good writing: brevity wins.
- *Michael Winter*

⌘

Writing is an exploration. You start from nothing and learn as you go. - *E. L. Doctorow*

COMMUNICATING IN WRITING AND THROUGH PRESENTATIONS

No audience ever complained about a presentation or speech being too short.
- *Stephen Keague*

⌘

The audience is likely to remember only three things from your presentation or speech. - *Stephen Keague*

⌘

We should just stop calling these things presentations altogether. Everyone gets hung up on that word. Wouldn't it be easier to just call them conversations? That's really what they are. - *Dale Ludwig*

⌘

During the first few minutes of your presentation, your job is to assure the audience members that you are not going to waste their time and attention.
- *Dale Ludwig*

⌘

Your slides should be a billboard not a document! - *Lee Jackson*

COMMUNICATING IN WRITING AND THROUGH PRESENTATIONS

> Simple and to the point is always the best way to get your point across.
> - *Guy Kawasaki*

⌘

> The first time you say something, it's heard; the second time, it's recognized; the third time, it's learned. - *John Maxwell*

⌘

> The first 30 seconds and the last 30 seconds have the most impact in a presentation. - *Patricia Fripp*

⌘

> Your ability to communicate with others will account for fully 85% of your success in your business and in your life. - *Brian Tracy*

What are your favorite quotations?

Why do these stand out for you?

Which would you want to adopt as your personal motto? Include on the signature line of your emails? Post on your desk?

COMMUNICATING IN WRITING AND THROUGH PRESENTATIONS

3

TIPS FOR AWESOME MANAGERS

As you review the following tips for communicating effectively, circle, check, or highlight those that are especially meaningful for you.

COMMUNICATING IN WRITING AND THROUGH PRESENTATIONS

Essentials of Professional Writing

1. **Determine the purpose of your message.** Ask yourself, "What is it that I'm really trying to say?" and "What do I want others to do after receiving my message?" It might help to imagine that you have only two sentences in which to convey your message: "The purpose of this email is to..." and "As a result of reading this email, I would like you to..." Rambling emails indicate that their writers didn't have a clear objective in mind. This leaves others confused and the message lost.

2. **Select an appropriate communication medium.** Before you even decide to convey your message in writing, ask yourself if this is the most appropriate medium in which to communicate your ideas.

COMMUNICATING IN WRITING AND THROUGH PRESENTATIONS

→ **Use verbal communication** for informal discussions, when no documentation is needed, and when an exchange of ideas is needed.

→ **Use written communication** when you need to provide information to people, keep information recorded for future use, emphasize your views or decisions, or have a reference for following directions.

→ **Use casual emails** for informal communications. They should be short and include an appropriate subject heading, a greeting, a closing, and, ideally, and an "Action Required" section.

→ **Use more formal letters** when communicating an official decision (letters of offer, contractual arrangements, etc.).

COMMUNICATING IN WRITING AND THROUGH PRESENTATIONS

3. **Develop an outline containing your key points.** This will help you identify your main point and the supporting points. Since people tend to remember what was said first and last, ensure that your strongest arguments aren't buried in the middle of your document.

4. **Employ Frank Hardesty's SPRA report format** when asking someone to take action.

   S – Situation (describe the situation)

   P – Proposal (describe your solution to the problem)

   R – Reason (explain your reasoning and rationale for your proposed solution)

   A – Action (indicate the action that you would like the recipient of your message to take)

   Your SPRA report should be brief and include headings so that readers can easily follow your reasoning.

COMMUNICATING IN WRITING AND THROUGH PRESENTATIONS

5. **Prepare and send a one-page monthly Good News/Bad News report to your manager.** According to Frank Hardesty, this is a quick way to keep your manager informed about your progress toward your goals and any snags along the way. It also serves as a helpful reference document for performance reviews.

6. **Write without stopping to edit or check your grammar.** This helps you get started with the process of writing rather than being paralyzed by a concern for correctness.

7. **Review and revise your draft.** Aside from the content issues just discussed and running a spell-check, evaluate the mechanics of your writing:
    → Words: Use language that is appropriate for the audience. For example, some occasions call for more

COMMUNICATING IN WRITING AND THROUGH PRESENTATIONS

formal language. Use simple words rather than complex ones. Sometimes people use complex words such as "utilize" instead of "use" because they think that it makes them look smarter. Unfortunately, when people come across challenging words, it takes them more time to process and understand these words, and this makes the message less efficient. Use jargon only if you're absolutely certain that your audience is familiar with it. Finally, be courteous and polite.

→ Sentences: Use the active voice whenever possible rather than the passive voice. For example, "I received your January 29th letter" is much easier to understand than "I am in receipt of your letter dated the 29th of January of this year." Also, avoid making your sentences complex. Ask yourself if there is a more direct and concise way

of expressing your thoughts.
- → Paragraphs: The first sentence should tell the reader what to expect in the paragraph. The body of the paragraph should be organized so that the transitions between the sentences flow naturally. The last sentence of a paragraph should summarize the main point of the paragraph. Cover only one topic in a paragraph. Each paragraph should be at least three sentences in length.

*Spelling and Punctuation

8. **Spell words correctly.** Examples:
    a. Achieve NOT acheive. Remember: "I before E except after C."
    b. Regardless NOT irregardless. The latter is not a word.

COMMUNICATING IN WRITING AND THROUGH PRESENTATIONS

9. **Use the appropriate words.** Examples:
   a. Manager NOT manger. Spell checks are unable to detect the inappropriate use of the word "manger."
   b. Moral vs. morale. Whereas "moral" refers to issues of right and wrong, "morale" refers to a person or group's level of enthusiasm or satisfaction.
   c. Advice vs. advise. Whereas "advice" is a noun (e.g., I am giving you advice), "advise" is a verb (e.g., I advise you to accept the offer).
   d. Effect vs. affect. Whereas "effect" is either a noun describing a result (e.g., The effect of the new policy was...) or a verb indicating cause (e.g., She effected a change in their opinions), "affect" is a verb meaning to influence (e.g., It is affecting my ability to drive carefully).
   e. Amount vs. number. Whereas the

words "amount" and "quantity" are used to describe quantities that are not easily measurable (e.g., amount of sugar), "number" is used when the quantities are discrete and countable (e.g., number of people or cars).

f. Less vs. fewer. Whereas the word "less" is used to describe quantities that are not easily measurable (e.g., less sugar), "fewer" is used when the quantities are discrete and countable (e.g., fewer people or cars).

g. Either/or and neither/nor. When you use the words "either" and "neither," be sure to use their appropriate companion words (e.g., Either project A or project B is acceptable. Neither project A nor project B is acceptable.)

h. Inferior to NOT inferior than. The word "inferior" should be followed by the word "to." (e.g., That proposal is inferior to this one.)

COMMUNICATING IN WRITING AND THROUGH PRESENTATIONS

i. Different from NOT different than. Remember that things are different <u>from</u> each other, not <u>than</u> each other. (e.g., That proposal is shorter than this one.)

j. Their vs. they're vs. there. Be aware of words that sound alike (homophones) such as these, and ensure that you use them correctly. (e.g., <u>Their</u> office is one floor up. <u>They're</u> happy people. <u>There</u> is a great leader.)

10. **Avoid clichés, euphemisms, and colloquialisms.** All of these tend to communicate your message indirectly (e.g., Use "He is assuming control of this project" rather than "He is taking the bull by the horns."). Instead of, "She got suckered by a conman," say "He manipulated her into..." Instead of "There's a lot of managers who care," say "Many managers care."

COMMUNICATING IN WRITING AND THROUGH PRESENTATIONS

11. **Avoid second-person pronouns** (i.e., you) unless appropriate. For example, instead of writing, "Electronic monitoring is sometimes used to control you," write "Electronic monitoring is sometimes used to control workers." Instead of writing, "My advice to managers is that you meet with your workers," write "My advice to managers is that they meet with their workers."

12. **Use gender-neutral language** wherever possible and applicable. Unless you are referring to a specific individual whose gender is known, use they/them/their. For example, instead of saying, "A manager should be friendly towards his workers" or "A manager should be friendly towards his/her workers," you could say, "Managers should be friendly towards their workers."

COMMUNICATING IN WRITING AND THROUGH PRESENTATIONS

13. **Use appropriate punctuation.**
    a. Apostrophe – Instead of writing, "the boys uncle," write the "boy's uncle." Instead of writing, "You can't judge a book by it's cover," write, "You can't judge a book by its cover."
    b. Comma – Instead of writing, "The office, described as bright and cheerful creates a feeling of warmth and friendliness," write "The office, described as bright and cheerful, creates a feeling of warmth and friendliness." Instead of writing, "This in addition to their frequent absence signals a lack of interest," write "This, in addition to their frequent absence, signals a lack of interest.

14. **Decide whether you will use American, Canadian, or British spelling, and use it consistently.**

COMMUNICATING IN WRITING AND THROUGH PRESENTATIONS

15. **Avoid redundant words** such as exact duplicate, absolutely essential, end result, exact same, added bonus or important priority. Replace them with duplicate, essential, result, same, bonus, or priority.

16. **Avoid missing words.** For example, people often omit the word "that" in a sentence (e.g., The documents she signed are here.).

17. **Avoid double negatives in a sentence.** (e.g. I don't want nothing. Instead, write: "I want nothing," or "I don't want anything."

***Flow**

18. **Structure paragraphs in a logical manner.** Ensure that your sentences build on each other rather than seeming to come out of nowhere. Use transitional

COMMUNICATING IN WRITING AND THROUGH PRESENTATIONS

words (e.g., although, as such, thus, moreover, but, furthermore, hence).

19. **Ensure that your sentences are concise and clear.** For example, instead of writing "This is a subject which usually holds much interest for teenagers," write "Usually, teenagers are interested in this subject."

20. **Use the active voice wherever possible.** "Be," "been," and "by" are a few signals of the use of the passive voice. Here are some examples of sentences written in the passive voice:
    a. Frankly my dear, a damn isn't given by me.
    b. She is seen as an empowering leader.
    c. He is considered to be an ethical decision maker.
    d. Several meetings have been held by our department.

COMMUNICATING IN WRITING AND THROUGH PRESENTATIONS

Here are the same sentences written in the active voice:

a. Frankly my dear, I don't give a damn. (from *Gone with the Wind*).
b. Workers see her as an empowering leader.
c. Others consider him to be an ethical decision maker.
d. Our department has held several meetings.

*Grammar

21. **Ensure that sentences are complete.**

22. **Avoid run-on sentences.**

23. **Ensure that the subject and verb agree.**
    Examples:
    a. The Rams are winning. [plural noun, plural verb]
       NOT: The Rams team are winning.

COMMUNICATING IN WRITING AND THROUGH PRESENTATIONS

   b. His bicycle, which was chained to the fence, and his jacket were both stolen.
   NOT: His jacket and his bicycle, even though he had it chained to the fence, was stolen.
   c. The team members disagreed among themselves.
   NOT: The team have disagreed among themselves.
   d. We each have our own responsibilities.
   NOT: Each of us have their own responsibilities.

24. **Avoid dangling phrases.** Examples:
   a. I donated my skis to Value Village.
   NOT: No longer used, I donated my skis to Value Village.
   b. I was able to buy the car for little money since it was rusty and six years old.

COMMUNICATING IN WRITING AND THROUGH PRESENTATIONS

    NOT: Being six years old and rusted through, I was able to buy the car for little money.

c. For sale by owner: 1978 Nova with manual transmission.
NOT: For sale, 1978 Nova by Owner with manual transmission.

d. I was on the way to the doctor in a vehicle that had rear end trouble when its universal joint gave way, causing me to have an accident.
NOT: I was on the way to the doctor with rear end trouble when my universal joint gave way causing me to have an accident.

e. His parents threw him out of the house when he turned 27.
NOT: On achieving the age of twenty-seven, his parents threw him out of the house.

COMMUNICATING IN WRITING AND THROUGH PRESENTATIONS

25. **Employ parallel structure.** Example:
    a. Managers were watch<u>ing</u>, read<u>ing</u>, and talk<u>ing</u>.
       NOT: Managers were watching, read the report, and talk about things.
    b. He was a handsome scholar.
       NOT: He was handsome and a scholar.
    c. His duties were preparing the agenda and calling the meeting to order.
       NOT: His duties were preparation of the agenda and calling the meeting to order.

26. **Ensure that the verb tense is consistent within a sentence and a paragraph.** E.g., "I searched the database and found..." rather than "I searched the database and I find that..."

COMMUNICATING IN WRITING AND THROUGH PRESENTATIONS

*Other Writing Tips

27. Use **bolding**, underlining, and UPPER CASE to draw attention to particularly important points but do so sparingly. To do otherwise makes YOUR document look **messy** AND confuses the **reader** (see?). Also, use one font (e.g., Times New Roman) and very few font sizes (e.g., 12 pt.). Avoid the CONTINUOUS USE OF UPPER CASE LETTERS because it comes across as shouting.

28. **If your document is two or more pages in length, number your pages.** The upper right-hand corner of the page is the standard location for a page number.

29. **Use appropriate margins** (generally about an inch on all sides).

COMMUNICATING IN WRITING AND THROUGH PRESENTATIONS

30. **Invest an hour in reading the classic book on effective writing: *The Elements of Style* by William Strunk and E. B. White.**

Essentials of Professional Presentations

*Preparation

1. **Determine the purpose of your message.** Ask yourself, "What am I really trying to say?" and "What do I want others to do after hearing my presentation?" It might help to imagine that you have only two sentences in which to convey your message: "The purpose of this presentation is to…" and "As a result of hearing my presentation, you will…" Are you hoping to simply inform your audience, or do you want to persuade them to take a particular action as a result of hearing your presentation?

COMMUNICATING IN WRITING AND THROUGH PRESENTATIONS

Are you hoping to inspire or entertain your audience? When people don't have a clear purpose in mind, they often deliver rambling and disorganized presentations. This results in a frustrated and bored audience and an unheard message.

2. **Know your audience**. You should know what information your audience already has so that you can build on this information. You should also know what their interests, concerns, and motivations are and customize your presentation to take these into account. Finally, if you're trying to "sell" something (a project, a plan, etc.), you should understand the possible advantages and disadvantages of it as well as the key objections that your audience is likely to have.

COMMUNICATING IN WRITING AND THROUGH PRESENTATIONS

3. **Prepare thoroughly for your presentation.** Off-the-cuff presentations usually lack both style and substance and are generally ineffective in motivating or influencing an audience. They also send the message that you didn't care enough about your message or the audience to invest time in preparation.

4. **Make good use of your presentation preparation time.** Your time is best spent developing the content and ensuring that the "meat and potatoes" are well developed. The sophistication of your presentation slides is secondary in importance. Put your effort into what counts the most: depth, insight, and well-developed ideas. In other words, ensure that you have something of substance to say before worrying about HOW you're going to say it.

COMMUNICATING IN WRITING AND THROUGH PRESENTATIONS

5. **Visualize yourself confidently making your presentation and responding to audience questions and comments.**

***Organization**

6. **Consider your content and its organization.** Prepare an outline of your main points and organize your presentation around these. Don't get lost in details that are interesting but not central to your message. Rather than simply talking about ideas, ensure that you use plenty of examples (personal or otherwise) to illustrate your points. Ensure that your presentation has a well-defined introduction, body, and conclusion. Your audience shouldn't have to guess what you're going to talk about next.

COMMUNICATING IN WRITING AND THROUGH PRESENTATIONS

7. **Have an attention-getting opening** such as some important statistics, a question, a quotation, an interesting story, or even some appropriate humor. Don't say, "I'm here to talk to you about..." Your opening should arouse interest, lead into the subject of your presentation, and set the mood. It shouldn't shock your audience. Here are three techniques:
   a. A challenging statement (persuade): Every one of us in this room has a problem.
   b. A quotation (inspire): Be the change you wish to see in the world (Gandhi).
   c. A mood setter (entertain): Once upon a time, in a land far away...

8. **Have a clear introduction** that communicates the purpose and organization of your presentation. Let the audience know when they can ask

COMMUNICATING IN WRITING AND THROUGH PRESENTATIONS

questions (at the end or throughout your presentation).

9. **Establish your credibility** with the audience by briefly sharing some information about your background and experience. If someone is introducing you, provide that person with a brief biography that contains pertinent information organized in a manner that allows that person to simply read from your biography.

10. **Ensure that the body of your presentation is well organized with a logical flow of ideas.** Don't jump from topic to topic in a disjointed manner with few links between ideas. This is especially problematic when several people must coordinate their efforts to make a single presentation. Here are five techniques:

COMMUNICATING IN WRITING AND THROUGH PRESENTATIONS

   a. Illustration: Suppose you had an experience like this.
   b. Describe an actual incident.
   c. Use a comparison or analogy.
   d. Offer and refute arguments that oppose your point of view.
   e. Quote an authority.
   f. Offer statistics (but be brief and concise).

11. **Cover a reasonable quantity of information,** given the time constraints. Don't try to make every possible point.

12. **Stick to one main topic** and develop it fully rather than covering a wide assortment of topics with little depth.

13. **Include triads, questions, and stories.** Triads – offering three ideas or examples – make ideas easier to understand and remember. This technique was used by

COMMUNICATING IN WRITING AND THROUGH PRESENTATIONS

both Winston Churchill and Margaret Thatcher. And you might recall Martin Luther King's famous words, "Free at last, free at last; thank God almighty, we are free at last." Questions increase involvement and help to structure your presentation. People often remember stories more easily than dry facts. As the saying goes, "Correlate, demonstrate, and illustrate!"

14. **Conclude with a summary of your key points and a "call to action."** This should answer the question "so what?" In other words, it should emphasize the relevance of what you were trying to say in your presentation to the audience. You should let the audience know what you would like them to do with the information you have presented. Here are three techniques:

    a. Summarize (effective for speech

COMMUNICATING IN WRITING AND THROUGH PRESENTATIONS

purpose "explain")
   b. Specific appeal for action (effective for speech purpose "persuade, inspire")
   c. Story, quotation, or illustration that emphasizes the point you have made (effective for speech purpose "persuade, inspire")

15. **Consider how your content is best delivered.** Most people find it helpful to use visual aids (PowerPoint slides, for example). They help the audience follow and focus on what you're saying remember your main points. But, don't read your slides or use them as a "crutch."

*Delivery

16. **Polish your delivery skills.** Although it isn't necessary or even desirable to memorize your speech, the best solution is to use your visual aids as a guide when

COMMUNICATING IN WRITING AND THROUGH PRESENTATIONS

you're delivering your speech. This eliminates the need for index cards and other papers that often only serve to distract people. Know your main points well enough that you only need to glance at a line on the screen as cue for what you're going to say. Practice making your presentation in front of others (family, friends, colleagues) who can give you helpful tips and suggestions. You may also find Toastmasters or the Christopher Leadership Course to be useful in building your self-confidence and skill in making presentations. Both offer established and proven programs delivered in a non-threatening, small group environment.

To find a Toastmasters' club near you, visit toastmasters.org. For information on the Christopher Leadership Course, visit clcnational.com.

COMMUNICATING IN WRITING AND THROUGH PRESENTATIONS

17. **Speak for the length of time that is expected of you.** Practice on your own so that you know exactly how long your presentation takes. "Be brief, be sincere, be seated," as Roosevelt recommended. Many good speeches are ruined by a meandering ending.

18. **Make eye contact** with those around you when you're presenting. Making eye contact is crucial to connecting with your audience. Try to maintain your eye contact for an entire sentence or thought. However, don't stare at individual audience members.

19. **Look around the room**, not just in one direction. Face all of your audience, not just people on one side of the room. Don't turn your back to them.

COMMUNICATING IN WRITING AND THROUGH PRESENTATIONS

20. **Use your voice.** Be enthusiastic about what you're saying. A monotone voice is monotonous for listeners. So, don't use a "reading voice," i.e. a fairly flat tone used when reading text. Without vocal variety, it sounds as though you're bored with your own presentation. Other tips:
    a. Know your material well enough so that you don't have to rely on your notes. This will allow you to speak more naturally in a conversational tone.
    b. Enunciate: pronounce words clearly.
    c. Speed: speak not too fast or slowly.
    d. Volume: speaking too loudly or too softly is uncomfortable for listeners.

21. **Don't look bored with your topic.** It bears repeating! Boredom shows up when you project low energy levels. You should try to be excited and proud about the work you've done. In other words,

COMMUNICATING IN WRITING AND THROUGH PRESENTATIONS

you should speak on a topic or issue that is of interest and importance to you. This will make your presentation a good experience for both you and your audience.

22. **Eliminate uhs and ums** and other verbal tics that distract from your message.

23. **Avoid distracting movements** such as frequently looking at your watch, jiggling change in your pocket, pacing, or wringing your hands.

24. **Use appropriate gestures.** If you're holding notes or cue cards, you won't be able to use many gestures in your presentation. You need to let go of the papers so that you can really emphasize your points with your gestures. Your gestures should be natural, not exaggerated. Here are some gestures to

COMMUNICATING IN WRITING AND THROUGH PRESENTATIONS

avoid:

a. Crossing your hands in front of you (fig leaf gesture). This makes you look nervous and timid.
b. Crossing your arms. This sends the message that you're unapproachable and closed to others' opinions.
c. Putting your hands in your pockets. This suggests nervousness, but it also may distract your audience if you're jiggling keys or change.
d. Pointing at someone, which comes across as aggressive.
e. Pulling at your ear, which is self-explanatory.

25. **Don't hold onto the podium for dear life.** You should step away from the podium and know your stuff well enough that you can rely on the slides solely as cues for what you're going to say.

COMMUNICATING IN WRITING AND THROUGH PRESENTATIONS

26. **Walk towards your audience**, if appropriate.

27. **Enjoy the experience**. Accept that being nervous is a normal part of making a presentation. Some nervousness can be a sign that you care about doing well. However, too much nervousness can keep you from focusing on getting your message across. Practicing your presentation in advance is helpful in this regard, as is trying some breathing exercises just before your presentation. Realize that people want you to succeed.

28. **Instead of hiding behind a "mask" of some sort, present your genuine self.** Projecting a fake image keeps people from getting to know you. Your audience will interpret your genuineness as sincerity, believability, and credibility – for both you and what you're saying. A good

exercise to see if "your image" is getting in your way is to stand up and say, "I'm glad to be alive" as loud as you can.

29. **Don't apologize** for your nervousness, the way you sound, your inexperience at making presentations, or anything else. This has the effect of redirecting your audience's attention away from the contents of your presentation to you as a presenter.

30. **Get the audience involved**, if possible and appropriate. You can do this by asking for a quick show of hands, using their names or other appropriate and relevant information, or asking questions that require brief responses.

COMMUNICATING IN WRITING AND THROUGH PRESENTATIONS

***Equipment/Visual Aids**

31. **Be prepared.** Know how the equipment works. Practice using similar equipment in advance of your presentation. Make sure that it is set up and functioning properly prior to your presentation, and ensure that any image that is being projected is sufficiently large for a person at the back of the room to see. Don't use up half of your presentation time trying to get the equipment to work. Similarly, ensure that your PowerPoint slides (if any) are loaded onto the computer used for the presentation well before your presentation.

32. **Don't use slides with small fonts that contain too much information.** Use slides for key words and points (an outline of what is said), not for the complete text to be read by a presenter.

COMMUNICATING IN WRITING AND THROUGH PRESENTATIONS

Use a font of 20 pts or larger. Adopt the 6 x 6 rule – 6 lines and a maximum of 6 words per line. Use an appropriate number of slides. Having too many slides will tempt you to rush through your presentation just to try to get through them all. A good rule of thumb is no more than 10 slides in a 15-minute presentation.

33. **Don't talk to or read off your slides**. Face the audience, and remember that your audience knows how to read. It's okay to refer to the slides occasionally, but you shouldn't be facing the screen throughout your presentation.

34. **Use a pointer** on your slides rather than your finger to direct attention to particular points.

COMMUNICATING IN WRITING AND
THROUGH PRESENTATIONS

4

DILEMMAS: WHAT WOULD YOU DO?

This section gives you the opportunity to consider how to apply what you've just learned to three exercises.

COMMUNICATING IN WRITING AND THROUGH PRESENTATIONS

Effective Writing

Imagine that you are the manager of 20 staff members. The WHMIS administrator has notified you that all staff must attend a training session on Workplace Hazardous Material Information Systems.

You have drafted the email on the following page to your workers. Make any necessary corrections and revisions to the email before turning the page.

COMMUNICATING IN WRITING AND THROUGH PRESENTATIONS

TO: All Staff
FROM: J. Ready, Manager
RE:

    I am in receipt of a email indicating employees must attend WHMIS sessions to be held on the following dates and times, location unknow at this point but will be announce as soon as it is determined by myself. On recieving this list, the WHIMIS program is very **important** so <u>please</u> pay ATTENTION to registering for it. You should review the list and signing for one the sessions not later than May 17 of this year.

May 20, 2:00 p.m. May 21, 7:00 p.m. May 22, 10:00 .

Signed, Cordially yours, ☺
J. Ready

COMMUNICATING IN WRITING AND THROUGH PRESENTATIONS

Have you revised the email? If not, please do so before reading the following text.

You have probably found that the draft email has several shortcomings. For example:
1. The dates should include the year.
2. A heading entitled "Re:" should be completed.
3. Although there is an attempt to motivate employees to attend the sessions, the message is getting lost in the poor spelling and grammar.
4. The memo employs run-on sentences, unnecessarily formal language, dangling phrases, and an excessive number of mechanisms for drawing attention (bolding, underlining, and upper case).
5. The signature line, "Signed, Cordially yours" with an emoticon, is not professional.

COMMUNICATING IN WRITING AND THROUGH PRESENTATIONS

Below is a revised version of the email that addresses the noted problems.

TO: All Staff
FROM: J. Ready, Manager
RE: WHMIS Training Sessions

Our administrator recently informed me that all staff must attend a WHMIS (Workplace Hazardous Materials Information System) seminar. These seminars are a great opportunity for all of us to refresh our knowledge of this important component of occupational safety. Please review the following list of seminar dates and times and, on the attached sheet, sign up for any one of them no later than May 17th.

> May 20, 2:00 – 3:00 p.m.
> May 21, 7:00 – 8:00 p.m.
> May 22, 10:00 – 11:00 a.m.

Best regards,
J. Ready

COMMUNICATING IN WRITING AND THROUGH PRESENTATIONS

Pre-Plan your Presentation

This exercise invites you to pre-plan your next major presentation. Plan your presentation according to each of the elements indicated below.

Prior to the presentation:

1. Purpose
    a. Theme, occasion
    b. Type of speech
    c. Main objective
    d. Desired audience actions after the presentation
2. People
    a. Audience: background, familiarity with topic, outlook, possible "enemies" and "friends"
    b. Size
    c. Expectations

COMMUNICATING IN WRITING AND THROUGH PRESENTATIONS

3. Place
    a. Location of the presentation
    b. Parking
    c. Equipment provided
4. Plan
    a. Agenda
    b. Where your presentation fits in the agenda, how much time you have for the presentation and questions
    c. Where you will sit
    d. Who is talking before you

Day of the presentation:

5. Placement
    a. Room – size, layout
    b. Seating
    c. Where you're presenting
    d. Lighting
    e. Sound system

COMMUNICATING IN WRITING AND THROUGH PRESENTATIONS

6. Paraphernalia
    a. Equipment
    b. Audio-visual
    c. Backup supplies
    d. Props
    e. Promotional materials
7. Person
    a. Image
    b. Being comfortable
    c. Projecting your voice

COMMUNICATING IN WRITING AND THROUGH PRESENTATIONS

Getting Used to Impromptu Speaking

Aside from preparing and practicing a presentation using the tips provided earlier, you may find it helpful to practice your impromptu speaking skills with a group of people. Here are two alternatives:

1. Progressive Story: The first person starts a story by contributing 2 or 3 sentences. The person to their immediate right then continues the story by contributing 2 or 3 sentences. This continues till everyone has participated. I did this exercise with a group of accounting professionals using the story of Goldilocks and the Three Bears as a jumping off point. The students were creative in developing the story in ways that no one could predict.
2. Table Topics: Everyone should write a topic on a piece of paper and put it in a bowl. The topics can be anything that you would like it to be, for example, your favorite

COMMUNICATING IN WRITING AND THROUGH PRESENTATIONS

vacation, your favorite meal, etc. The first person picks up a piece of paper and immediately starts talking about the topic that is indicated on that piece of paper for a total of two minutes (if possible). Then, the second person does the same, and so on. A version of this exercise is carried out at every Toastmaster's meeting. It's a great way of learning to speak on your feet in two minute chunks.

COMMUNICATING IN WRITING AND
THROUGH PRESENTATIONS

5

PLANNING FOR ACTION

In your learning journal, describe:

1. The top five challenges that you face in communicating in writing.
2. The specific actions you will take to address these challenges.
3. The top five challenges you face in making presentations.

COMMUNICATING IN WRITING AND THROUGH PRESENTATIONS

4. The specific actions you will take to address these challenges.
5. The lessons from this book that you could apply to these communication challenges.

COMMUNICATING IN WRITING AND
THROUGH PRESENTATIONS

About the Managerial Competencies Series

What's in the series?

This series is built around four managerial competency clusters: personal, people, purpose, and process.

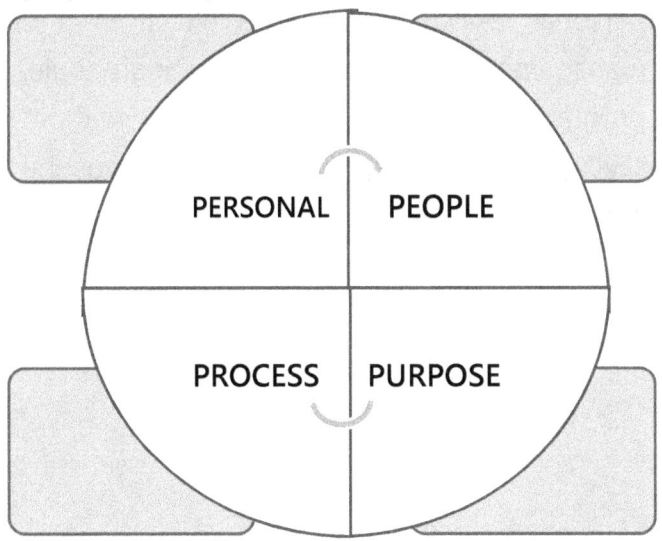

COMMUNICATING IN WRITING AND THROUGH PRESENTATIONS

Each cluster is made up of several competencies possessed by awesome managers. The series addresses a total of 15 competencies, each of which is the topic of a book of around 100 pages. Let's look at each cluster one at a time.

Personal Competencies

The starting point of the series is developing personal skills, given that effective self-management is essential for managing people, programs, and processes. It goes without saying that to manage others, you first must be able to manage yourself. People who are familiar with their personal strengths and challenges and who engage in effective self-management tend to work well with others.

COMMUNICATING IN WRITING AND THROUGH PRESENTATIONS

Here are the competencies included in the Personal Competencies cluster:

1. **Living the Core Values**, which involves demonstrating honesty, truthfulness, trustworthiness, reliability, fairness, and ethicality in all your decisions and interactions.
2. **Developing Personal Mastery** through personal responsibility, emotional resilience, constructive attitudes, self-confidence, adaptability, conscientiousness, and competence.

COMMUNICATING IN WRITING AND THROUGH PRESENTATIONS

3. **Organizing Yourself** by focusing on your priorities and making effective use of time.
4. **Building Stress Resilience**, which deals with managing life's stresses by developing personal hardiness.

People Competencies

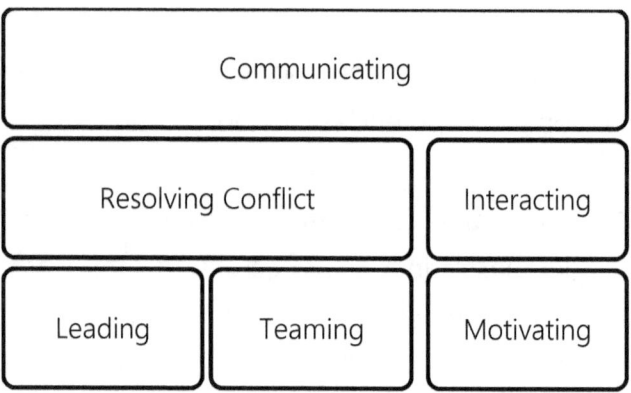

This cluster helps you examine and build your skills in working with and managing others. Although it's important for managers to be *technically* competent in order to gain credibility, interpersonal skills make the

COMMUNICATING IN WRITING AND THROUGH PRESENTATIONS

difference between awesome and not-so-awesome managers.

The competencies included in the People Competencies cluster are:

5. **Communicating in Writing and through Presentations**, which focuses on communicating ideas effectively, whether verbally or in writing.
6. **Creating Engagement**, creating motivating working conditions so that staff contribute their best to the organization.
7. **Building Relationships**, which considers how to interact with others through effective listening and responding.
8. **Resolving Conflict**, which addresses how to deal with conflict in a productive manner.
9. **Leading Your Team**, which means leading in a manner that is appropriate for the needs of the situation and your team.
10. **Cultivating Team Spirit** by building a cohesive, high-performing team.

COMMUNICATING IN WRITING AND THROUGH PRESENTATIONS

Purpose and Process Competencies

This final cluster combines two sets of competencies. Purpose competencies offer you a "big picture" perspective of your organization and your own role in the organization. Process competencies help you translate this "big picture" (the *whats*) into everyday practice (the *hows*). In other words, they allow you to consider how work should be done as a means of accomplishing the goals of your organization and your work unit.

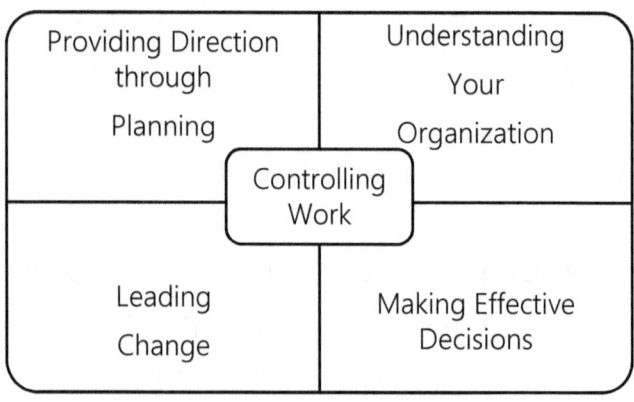

COMMUNICATING IN WRITING AND THROUGH PRESENTATIONS

Purpose and Process competencies include:

11. **Making Effective Decisions**, whether individually or in a team setting.
12. **Controlling Work Performance** by establishing control mechanisms to ensure results.
13. **Providing Direction through Planning**, which discusses the management process and offers tips for setting organizational direction and developing operational plans that fit this direction.
14. **Understanding Your Organization**, in other words, understanding the principles of organizing work and creating the right structure for your work unit.
15. **Leading Change** so that your organization and team thrive.

COMMUNICATING IN WRITING AND
THROUGH PRESENTATIONS

How is each book organized?

Each book is organized according to a five-step learning process. This process is designed to help you learn in an active and reflective manner.

In each book, after a brief introduction, we jump right into the "**reality check**." This series of self-coaching questions is meant to help you reflect on and develop insight into your own strengths and weaknesses in relation to a particular competence and, hopefully,

COMMUNICATING IN WRITING AND THROUGH PRESENTATIONS

motivate you to work on building your competencies.

The reality check consists of the kinds of questions that management coaches might ask you, but that you can simply ask yourself. Just be sure to give yourself a chance to answer them!

Management coaches help managers view and understand situations from a variety of perspectives. But, if the art of coaching is asking challenging questions (as management coach Chantal Binet says), why not ask yourself these questions?

Second, to accompany you on your learning journey, you're offered a curated collection of **inspirational quotes**. There's lots of wisdom available from people from all walks of life. The quotes that grab us and speak to us do so because they have touched a nerve in us. They resonate with us, perhaps because they offer a message that we need to hear to continue developing or because they challenge

COMMUNICATING IN WRITING AND THROUGH PRESENTATIONS

us to become better people.

Third, we offer you tons of **tips and tricks** of awesome managers. These practical tips cover a gamut of perspectives and actions that you can take to improve your competencies. Ideally, they will encourage you to consider the variety of possibilities and alternatives that are available to you. It's up to you to decide which are the most useful to you. As you read this section, be sure to note or highlight the tips that stand out for you.

Next, we present a series of **dilemmas** or situations for you to resolve. This section will help you see how you might apply the tips and tricks from the previous section. We ask you to read the situation and then identify what you would do in these situations. You might choose one of the alternatives that is offered, or you might come up with your own creative solution. Ultimately, there are many factors and perspectives that might influence what is the

COMMUNICATING IN WRITING AND THROUGH PRESENTATIONS

"best" choice.

Finally, we nudge you to develop an **action plan** that you will *actually* implement. Developing and implementing an action plan is an especially important step because it helps you draw value from your efforts in working through this series. After all, you're reading this book because you're hoping to become an awesome manager, right? This means developing a realistic plan that describes the actions that you intend to take to become an awesome manager, implementing your plan, reflecting on how well it worked, and then continuously making any adjustments that are needed. So, the cycle starts again!

COMMUNICATING IN WRITING AND
THROUGH PRESENTATIONS

How can you get the most out of the series?

You can read one or two books per month for an entire year, creating and implementing action plans for each book. Ultimately, this will help you develop a better understanding of yourself as a manager, your expectations, your strengths, and your areas for improvement.

As a way of refreshing your competencies, you can even re-read the books and re-visit your action plans in the future. Depending on what's happening in your life (new job, new team, new challenges), every time you read these books, you may develop new insights that help you deal with a situation.

COMMUNICATING IN WRITING AND THROUGH PRESENTATIONS

The knowledge of the world is only to be acquired in the world, and not in a closet.
Lord Chesterfield

What we have to learn to do, we learn by doing.
Aristotle

Life is a succession of lessons which must be lived to be understood.
Ralph Waldo Emerson

What do this British statesman from the 1600s, Greek philosopher from 384 B.C., and American poet from the 1800s have in common? They all agree that learning comes from trying new things, not from simply sitting back and reading a book.

Don't just read the books; *do* them! Just reading the books won't transform you into an awesome manager. If you just read the books, you might get to know a lot about what it

COMMUNICATING IN WRITING AND THROUGH PRESENTATIONS

means to be an awesome manager without changing what you do in the workplace. How useful is that? Just like learning to ride a bike, it's impossible to develop your skills by simply reading or even thinking about what you have read. Besides, as *The Matrix* reminds us, "There's a difference between knowing the path and walking it."

In order to truly learn from our experiences, we need to do a complete loop of the learning cycle: we need to reflect on our experiences, figure out what lessons we learned, consider ways to apply these lessons, and then apply them. You may know people who seem to repeat the same mistakes over and over again or people who continually approach situations in a manner that doesn't work for them. It's probably because they go through life without taking the time to reflect, consider what they've learned, and develop an action plan in order to change their experiences. They're stuck somewhere on the

COMMUNICATING IN WRITING AND THROUGH PRESENTATIONS

learning cycle. David Kolb, the creator of this learning cycle, says that we all have a favorite place on the cycle where we tend to get stuck.

Some people simply enjoy reading the books and reflecting on how they may relate to their lives, hopefully finding an opportunity to make use of their learning at some point in the future. However, without specific goals and action plans, they're not extracting as much value as they could from their investment of time and money.

Although this is partly due to differences in learning styles, it's also due to a reluctance to try something new and different. This may be caused by a fear of stepping out of one's comfort zone: what is familiar is comfortable. It may also be caused by a desire to accumulate a truckload of knowledge or have the perfect circumstances, such as the ideal boss or set of employees, before acting. Some of us think and think and continue to think without taking action. That used to be my

COMMUNICATING IN WRITING AND THROUGH PRESENTATIONS

personal downfall until I realized that knowing lots about a topic isn't the same as learning or making a difference in real life!

At the other extreme, some of us take action without first reflecting on our experiences and what we learned from them. Some people prefer to go ahead and try things out right away. They're more action-oriented than their reflective counterparts. These folks typically find it especially challenging to slow down, consciously reflect on what they're reading, and develop a well thought out action plan before acting. In the same way, if you just read the books and do nothing else, the learning process will get stuck right off the bat.

Reflecting and taking action is the best solution. It's not enough to *know* how to do something. Although it's helpful and important to take the time to reflect and develop insights, at some point, you need to *do* the work yourself. Otherwise, as management expert Peter Block has said, "Waiting becomes an

COMMUNICATING IN WRITING AND THROUGH PRESENTATIONS

excuse for not acting."

Here are **five other important things** to do to maximize your learning. First, **keep a learning journal**. Record your thoughts as you read the books, answer the self-coaching questions, and develop your action plans. It will help you clarify your thinking, see patterns in what you have been experiencing and writing, and serve as a record of commitments you have made to yourself through your action plans. You'll be able to look back at what you've written and be impressed with all that you've learned! You could use a notebook or create an electronic document. Some people even email journal entries to themselves as a way of recording the day and time of their entries.

Second, **pull together a feedback team** who can help you get the most from this series. Your feedback team could be a group of four or five people that you have confidence in, such as coworkers, your manager, friends,

COMMUNICATING IN WRITING AND THROUGH PRESENTATIONS

and family members. Don't be shy about asking people for their support in helping you become a better manager; they are more willing to help you than you might think! These discussions will offer you different perspectives and exponentially increase how much you learn from the series. Besides, awesome managers surround themselves with people they trust who are willing to give them honest feedback that will help them grow as individuals.

In supporting you, others can play one or more of the following roles:

→ The Head: These people can help you analyze a question or problem objectively. They can sketch out options, compare data, or simply provide you with accurate information.

→ The Heart: These people can help you express your emotions and understand them better. They listen, cheer you up, don't make judgments, and give you a

COMMUNICATING IN WRITING AND THROUGH PRESENTATIONS

sense of security.
→ The Legs/Arms: These people help you do things. They go places with you; they make you get moving when you don't feel like it. These people energize you.

How can your manager help? Can your manager provide feedback, advice and tips, and time to complete the series? What will you do to get your manager's help? For example, could you meet with your manager once every two weeks to discuss your progress and talk about how to manage effectively?

How can your peers help? Can your peers provide feedback, tips about managing, or coaching when needed? What will you do to get their help? Could you schedule a coffee break with them once every two weeks to discuss what you're learning and to share tips? Can you work through the series together?

How can your employees help? Can your employees provide feedback regarding

COMMUNICATING IN WRITING AND THROUGH PRESENTATIONS

your strengths and opportunities for improvement or work with you to develop a plan for making your unit function more effectively? What will you do to get their help? Could you meet with them once every two weeks to discuss what you're learning and how your team can implement elements of your action plan?

How can your friends help? Could they provide feedback, tips about managing, and encouragement for you to try new things? What will you do to get their help? Could you organize a dinner with them once every two weeks to discuss what you're learning and how to implement your action plan?

Third, **develop and implement a SMARTER action plan.** You know you've really learned something when your behavior changes (for the better, of course). Insights and tips that are

COMMUNICATING IN WRITING AND THROUGH PRESENTATIONS

meaningful to you will change your perspective *and* your behaviors. That's why each book ends by inviting you to develop an action plan. Your plan should be **Specific, Measurable, Attainable, Realistic, Timely, Exciting, and Rewarded.** Think about things that you need to start doing, stop doing, or continue doing. Here's an example: "By the end of next week, I will write two letters – one to my former manager and one to my best friend – expressing my gratitude for their coaching and willingness to challenge me to become a better person. I will send these letters by email no later than Friday afternoon." Write your action plan in your journal. Revisit it to check your progress, and revise your plan as needed. Remember to ask for help from others, evaluate your progress, and reward yourself for your progress toward becoming an awesome manager.

COMMUNICATING IN WRITING AND THROUGH PRESENTATIONS

Fourth, **identify obstacles or barriers that might get in your way of making the most of the series** and implementing your action plans; for example, lack of time or energy, poor personal habits, others' expectations, etc. List these in the column labelled "Obstacles" on the following page. Now, think about specific actions that you can take to address them and place these in the "Neutralizers" column; for example, meet with your manager, plan small wins or ways to celebrate your progress, etc.

COMMUNICATING IN WRITING AND THROUGH PRESENTATIONS

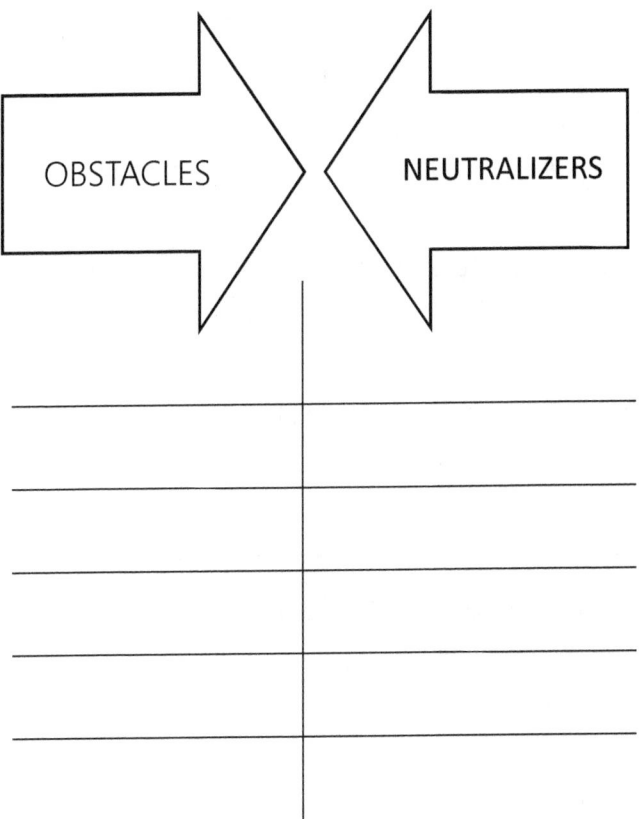

COMMUNICATING IN WRITING AND THROUGH PRESENTATIONS

Finally, do what you need to do to motivate yourself. Don't wait to be motivated to get started. Instead, get started, and motivation will come knocking at your door!

Also, try to be comfortable with discomfort. As you change how you manage, you may meet with some resistance from those around you. You exist in a system of relationships. Because systems are geared toward equilibrium (stability), if you change one thing in the system, the equilibrium is shot, and the system is upset. There may be pressure from others and from your own sense of comfort for you to do what you've always done regardless of whether or not it works.

It may be tempting to give up when things feel unnatural, but rest assured that this is part of the learning process. It's normal that trying out new ways of doing things makes you feel a bit uncomfortable in one way or another. Sometimes, we come across awesome folks who do their work without hesitation and

COMMUNICATING IN WRITING AND THROUGH PRESENTATIONS

seemingly without effort. It's easy to forget that they've gone through the highs and lows of the learning process. For example, think of Cirque du Soleil acrobats who seem to perform stunts with ease and pinpoint accuracy. It took them lots of practice, repetition, and even occasional failures to get to that skill level. Experts make things look easy.

Are you ready to begin your awesome journey? Earl Nightingale once said, "All you need is the plan, the road map, and the courage to press on to your destination." I hope that this series serves as your guide and road map on your journey toward awesomeness.

REFERENCES

Alessandra, T. & Hunsaker, P., (1993). *Communicating at work.* New York: Touchstone.

Hardesty, T. F. (no date). Action tools for increasing individual management productivity.

Strunk, W. & White, E. B., (1999). *The elements of style.* New York: Macmillan.

COMMUNICATING IN WRITING AND THROUGH PRESENTATIONS

Playbooks in the Managerial Competencies Series

1. Living the Core Values
2. Developing Personal Mastery
3. Organizing Yourself
4. Building Stress Resilience
5. Communicating in Writing and Through Presentations
6. Creating Engagement
7. Building Relationships
8. Resolving Conflict
9. Leading Your Team
10. Cultivating Team Spirit
11. Making Effective Decisions
12. Controlling Work Performance
13. Providing Direction through Planning
14. Understanding Your Organization
15. Leading Change

www.ingramcontent.com/pod-product-compliance
Lightning Source LLC
Chambersburg PA
CBHW070308230526
45470CB00002B/783